IN THE PALMS

OF THE

ALMIGHTY

By: Tiana Moore

IN THE PALMS

OF THE

ALMIGHTY

Copyright 2025 Tiana Moore
Published by:
Woman of Many Trades LLC

Story & Dedication

My name is Tiana Moore, and I was born on October 23, 1975, in Meridian, Mississippi, to my wonderful parents, Willie and Lizzie Moore. I am the baby of the family, blessed with siblings who mean the world to me: Inita, Anthony, Willie, and Candis. Before I gave my life to Christ, I was living in the world, clubbing, drinking, smoking, and doing things that were not pleasing to the Lord. But one day, I prayed sincerely, and God stepped in. He changed me for the better, gave me a new heart, and blessed me beyond measure.

Doctors told me I would never have children, but look at God! He gave me two beautiful blessings. Two mighty prayer warriors: my son, Willie H., and my daughter, Lizzie M.G. Truly, what a mighty God we serve! I want to acknowledge and give all glory to my

Lord and Savior, Jesus Christ. He has never failed me. He has pulled me out of situations I had no business being in, lifted me when I was down, and walked with me every step of the way. I am still a work in progress, but I am deeply in love with Jesus, and I look forward to seeing what He does next in my life.

Dedication to My Parents

A quote my mother wrote in her Bible: "Lord, love me enough so that your light shows up in me." This book is dedicated to my Daddy and Mother, Willie and Lizzie Moore, the two people who poured so much love, wisdom, and faith into my life. I could never ask for better parents. They showed me what true love looks like and how to worship and praise the Lord with all my heart.

My mother, Lizzie, was the very definition of a praying woman. Every night, without fail, she would kneel by her bedside and pray. Her love for her children was unmatched; she always told us she loved us, and even joked that she would only go to hell for us for three days. We would quickly rebuke that in Jesus' name and laugh together. That was Mama, full of love, humor, and faith. Although she is no longer with us on earth, her prayers, morals, and spirit live on in her children, grandchildren, great-grandchildren, and even great-great-grandchildren. I carry her memory in my heart, and I even named my daughter after her. Rest in peace, Mama. You were a mother in every sense of the word.

My father, Willie, is a man of quiet strength. He doesn't speak much, but when he prays, heaven listens. His prayers reach the throne room quickly and are answered with power. He has always had my back, sometimes even defending me when Mama was ready to discipline me. Daddy, I thank you for being steady, strong, and full of love. My son proudly carries your name.

My Siblings
My siblings are a blessing from God.

Inita, my big sister, practically raised me. She carried me on her hip and treated me like her own child. We were inseparable, and she has always been there for me in every season of life. Anthony, my oldest brother, is quiet, but our conversations mean everything to me. On the day of Mama's homegoing, we held each other and cried. With tears in his eyes, he reminded me, "We've got to take care of Daddy, just like Mama would want."

He has always been there when I needed him most. Willie, aka "Sip, my middle brother, now resting in peace, was with me for 13 years of my life. He had the best sense of humor, teased me like a brother should, and always showed me love. He even used to pay me and Candis to do his chores. I miss him dearly, but I carry his memory with me every day.

Katherine, my middle sister, who became an angel at birth. God called her home within minutes of her arrival. But I know heaven needed her more. Candis, my sister, has always been my protector. Mama told her, "Take your little sister with you," and she did. She fought my battles, included me in everything, and gave me a lifetime of memories full of laughter, love, and joy.

Troy, my sister Candis Husband. To me, he is not just an in-law; he is truly my brother, just like Anthony and Willie. He has been in my life since I was 11 years old, and from the very beginning, he treated me like his own sister. God didn't just give me two brothers; He blessed me with three.

My Children
My greatest blessings are my children.

My son, Willie, is named after his grandpa and uncles, and he came into the world with love overflowing. From the moment he was born, he wanted to be close to my heart, listening to my heartbeat. He has the most beautiful eyes, a tender heart, and a deep love for worship. From childhood, he has been drawn to sermons and worship music, and I know God's hand is on his life.

My daughter, Lizzie, named after my precious mother, was born by C-section. When the doctor placed her in my arms, she looked straight into my eyes with her blue eyes and blonde hair. She laid her tiny head on my chest as if to say, "I'm home." Lizzie is full of love, joy, and a deep passion for God. She prays and sings with all her heart, and she lights up every room she enters. She is truly my sunshine and a worshipper at heart.

As I write these words, tears fall because I feel the weight of love, loss, and blessing in my life. God has carried me through every season, from brokenness to redemption, from sorrow to joy, from being told "never" to seeing miracles with my own eyes. I thank God for my family, for every lesson, for every blessing, and for every prayer that has carried me. I am a work in progress, but one thing I know for sure: I am in love with Jesus, and He has never failed me.

TABLE OF CONTENTS

Strength in the Wait
DAY 1

Isaiah 40:31 "But they that wait upon the LORD shall renew their strength; they shall mount up with wings as eagles; they shall run, and not be weary; and they shall walk, and not faint."

Reflection: Waiting is not in vain. God strengthens those who wait with trust in Him. They shall mount up with wings like eagles. You will see the fruits of your labor. Be patient. Rest in the Lord and not in the issue. The issue will cause doubt, confusion, anger, and fear. Lean not on your own understanding, but lean and trust in the Lord your God.

Heavenly Father, I pray You renew my strength as I wait on You. Remind me that waiting is not wasted, but part of your preparation and divine timing. Give

---

me courage when fearful, strength when weakened and weary, and confidence when filled with doubt. Teach me to see this season as an opportunity to draw closer to You and to depend on Your unfailing promises. Teach me to see Your unconditional love. Anchor my soul in hope, knowing You will not fail me as I patiently and humbly wait on You. In Jesus' name. Amen.

Step of Faith: Write down one weary place in your life and cast your cares at the feet of the Father.

Trusting God's Timing
DAY 2

Ecclesiastes 3:1 "To everything there is a season, and a time to every purpose under the heaven."

Reflection: God's timing is always perfect, never rushed, or delayed. He will show up on time. Remember not to rush or get impatient with the process. You can never rush the hand of the Lord; trust in his perfect timing. Learn to have a posture of praise as you wait on the Lord. He will never stir you wrong. Trust in the Lord's timing.

Father, help me rest in Your perfect timing. I confess that I often want answers right away, and I can be impatient during the wait, but I know You see the whole picture while I see only fragments. Teach me how to wait and trust you wholeheartedly.

When discouragement settles in my heart, remind me that every delay is for my good and a form of protection. Help me to see Your favor of glory on my life. May I learn to walk at Your pace and not run ahead of You, losing sight of Your way. In Jesus' name. Amen

Step of Faith: Each time you feel anxious about when, or 'how,' whisper: 'God's timing is perfect.

Guarding Against Comparison
DAY 3

Hebrews 12:1–2 "(1)Wherefore seeing we also are compassed about with so great a cloud of witnesses, let us lay aside every weight, and the sin which doth so easily beset us, and let us run with patience the race that is set before us, (2)Looking unto Jesus the author and finisher of our faith; who for the joy that was set before him endured the cross, despising the shame, and is set down at the right hand of the throne of God."

Reflection: Comparison can be a distraction from the unique path God has designed for you. Never look at someone else's achievements with an envious eye, but seek the Kingdom of Heaven for God to show you who you are, and what He's assigned to your life. Look to God so you can focus and achieve what's to come next on your

---

special journey. Fix your eyes on the Lord even when it looks like you're losing the race.

Lord, protect me from the trap of comparison. Help me to focus on the race You have set before me instead of looking to the left or right. When I am tempted to envy, remind me of the blessings You have already given me. Fill my heart with gratitude and remind me that my worth is found in You alone. Let me celebrate others' victories while trusting that You are also writing my story beautifully. In Jesus' name. Amen

Step of Faith: Thank God today for three blessings in your life.

Faithful in Small Steps
DAY 4

Luke 16:10 "He that is faithful in that which is least is faithful also in much: and he that is unjust in the least is unjust also in much."

Reflection: Small acts of obedience in waiting seasons prepare you for greater things. Wait on the Lord and not on our own desires; our flesh speaks to us to surrender to God. Obedience is better than sacrifice.

Jesus, teach me to value the small steps of obedience. Help me to recognize that faithfulness in little things matters deeply to You. When I feel overlooked, remind me that You see every act of service and every step of obedience. Order my steps and shape my character in the quiet places so that I may be ready for greater responsibilities in Your Kingdom.

Step of Faith: Choose one small act of service to do today.

Praying First

DAY 5

Philippians 4:6-7 "Be careful for nothing; but in everything by prayer and supplication with thanksgiving let your requests be made known unto God. "And the peace of God, which passeth all understanding, shall keep your hearts and minds through Christ Jesus."

Reflection: Prayer guards your heart from anxiety and brings peace. Cast all your cares on the Lord, and surrender your whole heart to Him. He is the Prince of Peace and the refuge in the time of storm.

Lord, teach me to pray without ceasing before anything else. Too often, I rely on my own strength when I know my strength comes from You. Remind me of your word when it tells me, "the joy of the Lord is my strength." Remind me that your unfailing love casts out all my fears. I ask that You guide me in every decision. Fill my heart with peace as I lay my worries at Your feet. Guard my heart from fear, and remind me that You are always near, with Your ear inclined to my prayers, ready to respond with love. In Jesus' name. Amen.

Step of Faith: Begin your day with a short prayer before checking your phone or beginning any activities. Let your first thoughts be Christ and his goodness.

Listening Well
DAY 6

James 1:19 "Wherefore, my beloved brethren, let every man be swift to hear, slow to speak, slow to wrath."

Reflection: Waiting seasons are invitations to slow down and truly listen for God's voice. Focus and stand still, knowing that He is God, the King of Kings, the Lord of Lords, the Ruler over all of the earth. He will move on your behalf. Know God is in control.

Father, make my heart still enough to hear Your voice. Make my body still enough to be in your presence. Remove every distraction that keeps me from hearing you. Give me wisdom and knowledge to discern when You are speaking and courage to obey what You say. Help me to also listen to those around me with love and patience, reflecting Your heart in the way I respond to others. In Jesus' name. Amen.

Step of Faith: Take ten minutes of silence today to listen for God's whisper. Journal what you hear.

Serving Quietly
DAY 7

Matthew 6:4 "That thine alms may be in secret: and thy Father which seeth in secret himself shall reward thee openly."

Reflection: Quiet acts of service please God more than public recognition. Get into your prayer closet and pour out your heart. Ask Him to align your will with His. Ask Him to bless your hands so they may work diligently to please the Kingdom of Heaven. God hears your humble cry. He will catch every tear.

Lord, humble my heart so that I may serve with pure motives. Teach me to find joy in serving others without expecting anything in return. Let me reflect Your love through quiet acts of kindness. May my service point others toward You, not me, and remind me that

You see every hidden act of love. In Jesus' name. Amen.

Step of Faith: Do something kind for someone today without telling anyone, and say a prayer over the person you bless.

Joy in the Process
DAY 8

1 Thessalonians 5:16-18 "(16) Rejoice evermore. (17) Pray without ceasing. (18) In everything give thanks: for this is the will of God in Christ Jesus concerning you."

Reflection: Joy is not only in the outcome, but in the daily steps with God. Joy comes when you believe in God's promises and have faith in what He said. God will give you Unshakable joy, a deep spiritual satisfaction that the world can't supply.

Jesus, help me rejoice in the process, not only the destination. Even when progress feels slow, remind me that every step with You is meaningful, every lesson is meant to sharpen my discernment. Teach me to see joy in small victories and gratitude in daily blessings. May my heart remain light and thankful as I walk this journey with You. In Jesus' name. Amen.

Step of Faith: Write down three reasons you can be joyful for today. How can you spread the joy in your heart to others?

Peace While You Wait
DAY 9

John 14:27 "Peace I leave with you, my peace I give unto you: not as the world giveth, give I unto you. Let not your heart be troubled, neither let it be afraid."

Reflection: Peace isn't found in knowing the future, but in knowing Christ and God, which adds to every part of your life. Peace is the gift that the Prince of Peace has provided for us, knowing that He is the author and finisher of our lives.

Lord, You are my peace when my heart feels restless. Remind me that true peace doesn't come from having all the answers, but from abiding in You. Calm my anxious thoughts and guard my heart with Your presence. Anchor me in the truth that no matter what lies ahead, You are already there walking before me every step of the way. In Jesus' name. Amen.

Step of Faith: Each time you feel restless, take a deep breath and pray: 'Lord, thank You for being my peace.

Hope That Endures
DAY 10

Romans 15:13 "Now the God of hope fill you with all joy and peace in believing, that ye may abound in hope, through the power of the Holy Ghost."

Reflection: Hope in God keeps you steady when answers feel far away. Anchor yourself in the Lord, and God will keep you above water.

Father, fill me with hope that endures in the face of uncertainty. When doubt and discouragement try to take root, remind me that my hope is not in outcomes but in Your unchanging character. Help me to remember Your word when it says, "faith is confidence in what we hope for and assurance about what we do not see." Surround me with joy and peace as I am anchored in You, and let my hope overflow to encourage others who are waiting too. In Jesus' name. Amen.

Step of Faith: Write one area where you're losing hope. Speak God's promise over the situation you need God to breathe life into.

Becoming Who God Called Me to Be
DAY 11

Ephesians 2:10 "For we are his workmanship, created in Christ Jesus unto good works, which God hath before ordained that we should walk in them."

Reflection: Waiting is not about what you're waiting for, but who you're becoming while you wait. In your waiting season, have faith and trust in the Lord that you will see the fruits of your labor.

Lord, thank you that I am Your workmanship, created for good works that have been prepared in advance. Shape my character during this season of waiting. Remove anything in me that doesn't reflect You, and grow the qualities that do. Help me to embrace this process, knowing that You are preparing me for what's ahead. In Jesus' name. Amen.

Step of Faith: Ask God: 'What area of my character do You want to grow today?

Patience in the Process
DAY 12

James 5:7-8 (7) Be patient, then, brothers and sisters, until the Lord's coming. See how the farmer waits for the land to yield its valuable crop, patiently waiting for the autumn and spring rains. (8) You too, be patient and stand firm, because the Lord's coming is near.

Reflection: Just as a farmer waits for harvest, you must wait with patience and expectancy. Every seed that has been planted does not always produce a healthy plant unless you add fertilizer and water. As you grow, add the living water, which is Christ, to your seeds and watch with patience and see your Spiritual growth.

Jesus, I admit that I often want things quickly. Patience is a virtue, but teach me

---

to trust that good fruit takes time to grow. Help me to wait with expectancy, believing that Your promises will come to pass. Give me the grace to endure delays with peace, knowing that You are faithful to complete what You have started. In Jesus' name. Amen

Step of Faith: When impatience rises, breathe and repeat: "I will wait on the Lord."

Obedience Today
DAY 13

Deuteronomy 5:33 "Ye shall walk in all the ways which the LORD your God hath commanded you, that ye may live, and that it may be well with you, and that ye may prolong your days in the land which ye shall possess."

Reflection: God blesses daily obedience, even in the smallest steps. If you are faithful with little, you can be trusted with much. Ask the Lord to help you steward what He's blessed you with.

Prayer: Father, give me a willing and obedient heart. Help me to walk in the path You've set before me, step by step. Even when I don't understand the full picture, remind me that obedience brings blessing. Give me courage to obey quickly and joyfully, knowing that each step matters to You while we walk in obedience. In Jesus' name. Amen.

Step of Faith: Choose one area where you can obey God today without delay. Write a prayer of surrender.

God's Plans are Good
DAY 14

Jeremiah 29:11 "For I know the thoughts that I think toward you, saith the LORD, thoughts of peace, and not of evil, to give you an expected end."

Reflection: Even when unclear, God's plans are always for your good. God's plan is to prosper us and not harm us; hold on to His unchanging hand.

Lord, I trust that Your plans for me are good, even when I cannot see them clearly. When I feel uncertain, help me to rest in the truth that You have a future filled with hope prepared for me, a future meant for a prosperous end. You did not give me a spirit of fear with your assurance. I know that You are guiding every detail of my life for my good and Your glory. In Jesus' name. Amen.

Step of Faith: Speak Jeremiah 29:11 over your life today. Write down the plans God has for your life.

Anchored in Christ
DAY 15

Scripture: Hebrews 6:19 "Which hope we have as an anchor of the soul, both sure and steadfast, and which entereth into that within the veil;"

Reflection: Jesus is your anchor when storms and waiting seasons come. Use your anchor and make sure your boat is secure. Don't have unwavering faith. Prayer will build unshakeable faith.

Lord, thank You that my hope in You is an anchor for my soul. When the winds of uncertainty blow and waves of doubt rise, keep me steady and secure in You. Help me to cling to Your promises and to trust that You will never let me drift away. Help me to trust that in the palms of your hands, I am anchored deeply in your love and truth. In Jesus' name. Amen.

Step of Faith: Draw an anchor symbol and write: 'My hope is in Christ.

Faith Over Fear
DAY 16

2 Timothy 1:7 "For God hath not given us the spirit of fear; but of power, and of love, and of a sound mind."

Reflection: Fear grows in waiting seasons, but faith silences fear. The "what if" doesn't doubt God; he didn't give you a spirit of fear, He is not the author of confusion, and He is not a man who should lie.

Father, replace my fear with faith today. When I feel afraid of the unknown or anxious about the future, remind me that You have given me power, love, and a sound mind. Strengthen my spirit so that I may walk boldly in faith, knowing that You are with me and will never leave me. Help me to remember in my times of doubt and trouble not to fear because

You are with me and my help comes from You. Help me to remember I am upheld in your righteous right hand. In Jesus' name. Amen.

Step of Faith: Identify one fear and speak God's truth against it. "I am fearfully and wonderfully made."

Daily Bread
DAY 17

Matthew 6:*11* "Give us today the food
we need,"

Reflection: God provides what you need
daily, not always in advance, but always
on time. Don't worry if God provided
manna and quail every day for the
Israelites, He will provide for you daily.

Lord, thank You for providing my daily
bread. Even when I want to see the
whole plan, remind me that You supply
my every need daily. Help me to be
grateful for today's provision and trust
You for tomorrow's needs. Teach me to
rest in Your faithful care and not worry
about what tomorrow brings. In Jesus'
name. Amen.

**Step of Faith: Write three ways God
has provided for you recently.**

Humility in Waiting
DAY 18

1 Peter 5:6 "So humble yourselves under the mighty power of God, and at the right time he will lift you up in honor."

Reflection: Humility means surrendering your timeline to God's authority. Let go of things that you have planned. Things will not always happen the way you planned. Be patient and wait on the Lord.

Lord, help me to humble myself. Teach me to surrender my own plans and trust in Yours. When I am tempted to push forward in my own strength, remind me that true blessing comes from waiting on You. Give me a heart of humility that bows to Your wisdom and timing. In Jesus' name. Amen.

Step of Faith: Say aloud: 'God, I trust Your timing more than mine. "Step of Faith: Say aloud: 'God, I trust Your timing more than mine."

Perseverance Builds Character
DAY 19

Romans 5:3-4 (3) We can rejoice, too, when we run into problems and trials, for we know that they help us develop endurance; (4) And endurance develops strength of character, and character strengthens our confident hope of salvation.

Reflection: Trials and delays refine your character and deepen your faith.
Adversity proves our faith, our endurance has time to grow, soon.
Maturity comes.

Father, thank You for using waiting seasons to strengthen me. Though trials are not easy, I trust that they are producing endurance and building my character. Help me to rejoice even in challenges, knowing they are shaping me into someone more like Christ. Give me perseverance that endures with joy. In Jesus' name. Amen.

Step of Faith: Write down one way God has used waiting to shape your character.

Walking By Faith
DAY 20

2 Corinthians 5:7 "For we live by believing and not seeing."

Reflection: Waiting requires walking by faith, not by what you see. The Holy Spirit within you will guide you in determining your actions if you only ask. He will reveal beyond what you hear or see.

Jesus, help me walk by faith and not by sight. When the way ahead is unclear, remind me that I don't need to see the full path to take the next step with You. Strengthen my trust in Your promises and help me rely on Your presence to guide me, even when I cannot see the outcome. Help me to develop steadfast faith with a posture of praise as I wait for your hand to move. In Jesus' name. Amen.

Step of Faith: Step into one thing today that requires faith, not sight.

Worship While You Wait
DAY 21

Psalm 34:1 "I will praise the Lord at all times. I will constantly speak his praise."

Reflection: Worship lifts your focus from your waiting to your faithful God. By choosing worship, we put God in the center. Our concerns are now in God's hands. Remember, He can do all things, and He can never fail.

Lord, let worship rise from my heart, and the praise from my lips be acceptable in your sight in every season. Even when I am waiting, help me always to bless Your matchless and holy name. Shift my focus from what I lack to who You are, which is the beat of my heart and the breath in my lungs, and my first love. Let my worship be a weapon against discouragement and a declaration that I trust You no matter what. In Jesus' name. Amen.

Step of Faith: Play one worship song and sing it as a declaration.

God Works in the Waiting
DAY 22

Romans 8:28 "And we know that God causes everything to work together for the good of those who love God and are called according to his purpose for them."

Reflection: Even when you can't see it, God is working all things together for your good. The Glory of God shines upon us, his redeeming work. God's children encounter the divine image within themselves.

Father, thank You that even in silence, You are at work. When I cannot see progress, remind me that You are arranging everything for my good. Strengthen my faith to trust that You never waste a season of waiting. Fill me with peace, knowing You are working behind the scenes on my behalf. In Jesus' name. Amen.

Step of Faith: Thank God for one unseen way He may be working in your life.

Strengthened by His Word
DAY 23

Psalm 119:105 "Your word is a lamp to guide my feet and a light for my path."

Reflection: God's Word gives us light for the next step when the future feels foggy and unsure. When we face what we can't see, it can be mind-blowing, but God's protection guides our next steps, removing fear with faith. It will take you in the right direction.

Lord, thank You for the light of Your Word. When I feel lost or unsure, remind me that Your Word is a lamp to my feet and a light to my path. Teach me to lean on Scripture daily for wisdom and direction. Your word ensures me You will instruct and lead me everywhere I go. Let Your truth guide my choices and bring clarity where there is confusion. In Jesus' name. Amen.

Step of Faith: Read one Psalm slowly aloud and write down what stands out.

Endurance in Prayer
DAY 24

Luke 18:1 "One day Jesus told his disciples a story to show that they should always pray and never give up."

Reflection: Jesus said to pray and not give up; persistent prayer builds faith. Praying without ceasing turns every predicament and occasion into fellowship.

Father, give me endurance in prayer. When I feel like giving up, remind me of the widow who persisted and received justice. Strengthen my faith to keep asking, seeking, and knocking, trusting that You hear every prayer. Help me to stay consistent in bringing my needs before You, even when answers feel delayed. In Jesus' name. Amen.

Step of Faith: Revisit one unanswered prayer. Pray over it again today.

God's Faithfulness Never Fails

DAY 25

Lamentations 3:22-23 (22)The faithful love of the Lord never ends! His mercies never cease. *(23)* Great is his faithfulness; his mercies begin afresh each morning.

Reflection: God's mercy is new every morning; He is always faithful. God's love and faithfulness never run out, so we should feel His love every day. Besides our weaknesses and flaws, we can always depend upon Him.

Lord, thank You for Your great faithfulness. Even when I have failed, Your mercy has met me every morning. Remind me of the countless ways You have provided, protected, and guided me. Help me to live with confidence in Your unchanging nature, knowing that You are the same today as You were yesterday

and will be forever. In Jesus' name.
Amen.

Step of Faith: List three times in your past when God proved faithful.

Courage to Keep Going
DAY 26

Joshua 1:9 "This is my command, be strong and courageous! Do not be afraid or discouraged. For the Lord your God is with you wherever you go."

Reflection: God's presence gives us the courage to endure long seasons of waiting. The way we can survive long waiting seasons is to lean and depend on God, step aside and let him work in the background, and be patient. Patience is a virtue.

Father, give me the courage when I feel like throwing in the towel. Remind me that You are with me every step of the way, and I have nothing to fear. Strengthen my heart to be bold and steadfast, even when the road feels long.

Let me walk forward with confidence, knowing that Your presence surrounds me always. In Jesus' name. Amen.

Step of Faith: Declare this verse aloud: 'God is with me wherever I go.

Contentment in All Seasons
DAY 27

Philippians 4:11-12 "Not that I was ever in need, for I have learned how to be content with whatever I have. I know how to live on almost nothing or with everything. I have learned the secret of living in every situation, whether it is with a full stomach or empty, with plenty or little."

Reflection: True contentment comes from Christ, not circumstances. God's strength and peace can handle any situation. We have to have faith in Him to handle it for us.

Jesus, teach me to be content in every season. Whether I have much or little, let my heart rest in You. Free me from the trap of discontentment and fill me with gratitude for what I already have. Let me find my joy in You alone, knowing You

are my greatest treasure. In Jesus' name.
Amen.

***Step of Faith: Thank God today for
what you already have.***

Steady Hope
DAY 28

Psalm 62:5-6 (5) "Let all that I am wait quietly before God, for my hope is in Him. (6) He alone is my rock and my salvation, my fortress where I will not be shaken.

Reflection: Hope in God brings steadiness, even when life feels uncertain. God is in control; we must anchor ourselves in Him and sit back, waiting for the storm to pass. He will weather it.

Lord, be my rock and my salvation. When everything around me feels unstable, remind me that You are unshakable. Teach me to place my hope firmly in You so that I will not be moved by fear or doubt. Let my soul find rest and strength in Your presence alone. In Jesus' name. Amen.

Step of Faith: Write this verse and place it somewhere you'll see daily.

Becoming Rooted
DAY 29

Colossians 2:6-7 (6) And now, just as you accepted Christ Jesus as your Lord, you must continue to follow him. (7) Let your roots grow down into him, and let your lives be built on him. Then your faith will grow strong in the truth you were taught, and you will overflow with thankfulness.

Reflection: Waiting seasons deepen your roots in Christ. It's not a delay; it's equipping you to handle the big situation and the favor God has in store for you.

Father, root me deeply in Christ so that life's challenges will not sway me. Teach me to grow strong in faith and overflowing with thankfulness. In this waiting season, help my roots go deeper into Your love, so that I may stand firm and bear fruit for Your glory. In Jesus' name. Amen.

__Step of Faith: Spend 10 minutes journaling about how God is growing your roots.__

Rejoicing in Advance
DAY 30

Habakkuk 3:17-18 (17) Even though the fig trees have no blossoms, and there are no grapes on the vines; even though the olive crop fails, and the fields lie empty and barren; even though the flocks die in the fields, and the cattle barns are empty, (18) yet I will rejoice in the Lord! I will be joyful in the God of my salvation!

Reflection: Even before the breakthrough comes, you can rejoice in God. When you praise God in advance, it shifts the ambiance, preparing the way for requests to be granted.

Lord, give me the faith to rejoice even before I see the answer. Remind me that my joy is not dependent on circumstances but on who You are. Help me to praise You in advance, declaring that You are faithful. Let my worship rise as an act of trust that You will come through in Your perfect way. In Jesus' name. Amen.

Step of Faith: Praise God today for what you're still waiting on.

The Reward of Waiting
DAY 31

Isaiah 64:4 "We are all infected and impure with sin. When we display our righteous deeds, they are nothing but filthy rags. Like autumn leaves, we wither and fall, and our sins sweep us away like the wind."

Reflection: God acts on behalf of those who wait for Him. Your waiting is not in vain. God is shaping and molding us for His glory. We can't see him working, but we must trust his process, and God is never wrong. We must submit to him wholeheartedly.

Father, thank You that You reward those who wait on You. Remind me that my waiting is never wasted and that You are always working for my good. Give me patience to trust the process and faith to believe in Your promises. At the end of this journey, may I see how You have been faithful every step of the way. In Jesus' name. Amen.

Step of Faith: Celebrate today by thanking God for how He's been with you this whole month.

The Lord is our Strength

walk the right path and grow stronger in my faith. Through prayer and encouragement, my dear sister in Christ, Ebony Brinson, has inspired me to step out in obedience and write this 31-day devotional before the release of my larger book. This devotional is not just words on paper; it is a daily guide designed to help you draw closer to Christ, to seek His face in every season of your life, and to strengthen your walk with Him.

My prayer is that each devotion will touch hearts deeply, both believers and those still searching for truth. I pray it stirs a hunger within you to spend time in God's presence, to lean on His promises, and to understand the power of His Word. May every page encourage you to press forward on your spiritual journey, knowing that God's love is unfailing and His grace is enough.

Lord, I lift this devotional up to You. May it be a vessel to bring Your people to Your feet daily. May it draw them into a deeper relationship with You, giving them strength, peace, and hope to endure. Let it inspire transformation, renewal, and healing for all who read it.

This devotional is not just the beginning of a book, but the beginning of a deeper walk with Christ. My prayer is that it will remind you that no matter where you are in life, God is waiting with open arms to lead, guide, and restore you.

Everyone has a story, but you don't need to spend your life striving for traditional publishing. Rejection doesn't have to be your path; you don't have to shoulder all the work while publishing companies reap the rewards. There's a thriving community of independent authors, just like you, who are successfully publishing their stories and making a living. Our technological expertise can make the journey to publication a breeze. Let Woman of Many Trades LLC handle the challenging aspects, allowing you to focus on your writing.

Send us your Word Document, and we'll cover the rest. It's that straightforward! Traditional publishing houses often prioritize "celebrity authors" over the everyday writer, making it nearly impossible for first-time authors to break through. However, the landscape has evolved, and self-publishing is now a viable and respectable option. It's no longer considered "vanity publishing." The self-publishing industry empowers authors to get their work published quickly, retain their rights, and earn up to ninety percent of their royalties, a substantial increase from the traditional five to seven percent.

Woman of Many Trades is a versatile and multifaceted business offering a variety of services. Our primary objective is to provide a service that alleviates your needs, whether creating distinctive business logos, crafting compelling written proposals, or assisting with self-publishing. Do you genuinely want to invest all your time in the tedious tasks of formatting, converting, and designing a book cover, not to mention the laborious process of self-promotion? Our team of professional editors is here to relieve you of these burdens.

We genuinely hope you'll embark on becoming a published author and part of our expanding Woman of Many Trades family. May you achieve the global recognition you rightfully deserve. You are deserving of success. Remember, success belongs to those who create opportunities, not those who wait for them. Have faith in yourself and believe in your ability to accomplish anything, as it all begins with the power of your mind. Thank you for choosing to join us on your adventure to success!

www.womanofmanytrades.com
www.instagram/woman_ofmany_trades7
www.facebook.com/womanofmanytrades

Stay Connected

Thank you for taking the time to read *In the Palm of the Almighty*. Your support means so much! Stay connected with **Tiana Moore** for upcoming books, devotionals, and inspiring messages that uplift the soul and empower your walk with Christ to strengthen your faith.

https://www.facebook.com/tiana.love.5
https://www.youtube.com/@Prayerwarrior4517
https://www.instagram.com/lovingwillie67/
https://www.tiktok.com/@_chosentee

Join the community of believers growing in faith, purpose, and peace, because when you rest in the palm of the Almighty, your story continues to unfold with grace.